CW00741551

ELEMENTAL LIVING

ELEMENTAL LIVING

CONTEMPORARY HOUSES IN NATURE

Designing homes for natural environments often presents a paradox: how, when most construction systems are inherently geared towards both speed and efficiency, can the act of building align to the rhythm of the landscape? While processes we commonly associate with the natural environment—erosion, weathering, and patination, for example—are far more gradual, the pace with which we build is on an exponential rise.

That said, we have an inherent yearning to retreat. As the world continues to urbanize and our feeling of isolation from the "natural world" grows, our desire for a place away from the milieu of city life increases. Many of those who can afford to build a getaway recognize the fundamental responsibility that comes with it: a duty to enhance, as opposed to blight, the landscape in which it is set.

Building is often seen as a harmful process in these types of settings, but, while this is often true, there are exceptional cases. This book collects projects of this kind; those that, because of either the deferential approach of the architects and their clients or the demands from the landscape itself, engage with their surroundings in an innovative and considered way. The first section highlights houses built within nature—structures that respond to a particular context, such as a woodland, a valley, or a cliff face, by employing materials that can be extracted, harvested, or found nearby in order to blend into the landscape. The second section is a collection of projects designed for the purpose of looking at nature: houses in which certain elements, such as windows, terraces, and platforms, are specifically positioned to command spectacular views. The third section explores how nature itself becomes an active building element, either because the construction materials were taken directly from the surroundings or because the topography of the site is a part of the structure, driving the shape of the building.

These are buildings that embody a profound awareness that dwelling can be far more than simply residing. Interaction between the artificial and natural can be achieved with patience and (local) knowledge. A structure's short-term impact on the land can therefore be minimized, and its long-term stability can ultimately be preserved.

Architects who embrace nature, and especially those who push the boundaries of what is materially possible, deserve to be celebrated. The residences gathered here—from Indian houses to Swedish cabins and even a Japanese treehouse—are defined by a certain sensibility that manifests itself, often with exceptional beauty, in an architecture that is in conversation with its context.

[1] BUILT TO LOOK AT NATURE

One of architecture's fundamental roles is to present, and represent, the world around us. Its simplest elements—walls, roof, windows, door—serve to bridge interior worlds, or rooms, with exterior space, a role that gradually, as technologies have evolved alongside new types of craftsmanship, has assumed greater importance to those who wish to dwell poetically.

Today, buildings that truly engage with nature on this level are more difficult to find. A fine line exists between those that simply speak to their surrounding landscape, and those that both speak *and* respond to it. Dialogue, in this sense, is elementally important; without it, architecture can feel both anachronistic and out of touch. The best projects tend to offer a constellation of moments—threaded to form a coherent whole—that mirror habitual rituals and individual patterns of living. It is here that the landscape is either drawn inward or the inhabitant is encouraged to look outward, and, as a result, a building is able to engage holistically with its environment.

Framing the landscape is a commonality in contemporary architecture, and even more so when a house is located in an exceptional natural environment. The ways in which such buildings interact in such settings is a more complex practice, requiring a comprehensive understanding of geography and climate that can be applied to space and openings. Often it is not the most obvious view that becomes the most intriguing; architectural geometries and tectonics can be used to highlight striking vistas that can only be established through design. Landscapes can be inventively framed, which is an integral aspect of looking at—and interpreting—nature.

These projects might be considered "withdrawn"—buildings that protect themselves from the outside world yet remain able to intelligently frame it; or "open"—houses that encourage a more direct interaction with their landscapes. Both types, as can be seen in this chapter, have the potential to create quite astonishing, and timeless, architecture.

Situated on the Atlantic coast of the Iberian Peninsula near the Spanish city of Cádiz, Alberto Campo Baeza's House of the Infinite is radical in its formal composition; when viewed as an element both in and of its surrounding landscape, it is particularly striking. The building both opens out onto the immense ocean horizon and provides shelter from the strong prevailing winds. Defined by its smooth, flat roof plane, which accommodates a pool, a collection of light wells, and access to the rooms below—it is a structure that attempts to epitomize the maxim "nothing more and nothing less."

At the base of the building, warm white sand meets a wide patio of Roman travertine—a stone that directly references the city's Ancient Roman antecedents. Carved from a rocky outcrop that ascends gradually from the flat sandy shore to the dunes and greener banks beyond, the minimalist frontage of the house belies a more complex interior arrangement. At 118 feet (36 meters) deep, the living space is clean, bright, and white. Large windows look out onto the seemingly infinite seascape beyond. The sensitive material choices recall a time long lost: when Ancient Romans fished the waters and the offshore winds carried the Ancient Greeks of mythology and folklore.

Located on a gracefully landscaped crest at the edge of Philip Johnson's estate in New Canaan, Connecticut, the Glass House represents the first of fourteen experimental "essays" the architect designed and built between 1949 and 2005. The single rectangular room, enveloped fully in glass, is defined by its transparency and simple, precise geometries.

Incorporating just three core elements—a flat steel roof; a shallow, brick plinth; and a cylindrical brick hearth, which also accommodates the bathroom—the house translates and amplifies contextual motifs into abstract structural components. The surrounding grounds, cultivated by Johnson and his partner, David Whitney, over the course of their lifetimes, oscillates between "vestibules" of trees and grassy clearings, recalling the *faux-naturale* articulation and boundless horizons of the informal eighteenth-century English garden.

Although innovative for its time, the pavilion's experimental design necessarily sacrifices functional qualities for aesthetic purity. Perhaps the most telling attestation to its environmental performance is that its architect eventually occupied the building only when entertaining guests.

Pika House is set on a steep hill in a dense woodland of tall spruce trees in Dunton Hot Springs, Colorado. Designed to fit a relatively small footprint, the house rises five stories to capture views across the forested landscape and Dolores Peak in the Rockies beyond.

The kitchen and dining room are located on the first floor, with the living room and library on the second. The two floors above contain bedrooms and bathrooms, and a penthouse study surrounded by a roof deck crowns the tower, just shy of the treeline. Constructed with a steel frame, the house is paneled in Spanish cedar and recycled Douglas fir. When not in use, the entire house can be sealed shut with dark aluminium shutters, providing protection from snow and harsh winter light.

Located in Sydney's Dover Heights, Holman House perches precariously over the edge of a 230-foot (70-meter) cliff above the Tasman Sea. The curvilinear form of the building, inspired by Pablo Picasso's 1928 painting *The Bather*, fluidly expands and contracts to direct views of the surrounding cliffs and across the water in all directions. In the interior, the living spaces have been adapted to the meandering perimeter, its apertures positioned in response to the movement of the sun throughout the day.

The living and dining areas cantilever over the water, supported by a series of slender columns. This volume is anchored to a base constructed from rough stone, designed to appear as though it were an extension of the rock face below. These walls continue around the property, converging to create a series of terraces that accommodate gardens and a pool.

This house, composed of two built elements and a court-yard in between, is set within a grand, undulating land-scape. Framing views in every direction, the building is designed to directly engage with the peaks of the surround-ing mountain ranges, its angled roofline mirroring the slopes. The wooden ceiling rafters inside expand on this sensibility, both perspectively and aesthetically, by draw-ing the eye down and out to the extensive terrain.

The large, tapered living spaces are composed of mate-rials that complement the natural landscape. The moun-tains, covered in sagebrush, are grazed each morning by the sun. All sense of scale falls away, and the monolithic mass of a house begins to feel minuscule within the set-ting—it is a perfect portal through which to observe, and admire, the power of the natural environment.

Richard Meier's Douglas House, completed in Harbor Springs, Michigan, in 1973, is a four-story residence anchored to a steep slope. Built of steel and wood, and painted a stark white, the house is an abruptly visible element within the surrounding forested landscape. Large windows wrap around the building, showcasing panoramic views of the valley and hills beyond while bringing bright light into the open collection of interior spaces.

The architect describes the house as a machine-crafted object that appears to have landed in a natural world. Its color, one of its most distinguishing features, gives it a highly assertive presence; it is enhanced by contrasting with its surroundings. The whiteness persists in the interior. Divided into two zones, public spaces and those that are private, the house has large living areas and smaller, more intimate sleeping accommodations. From the outside, this division can be discerned by the size of the windows: large for public, small for private.

Evident upon first glance, this house is a powerful, simple structure. Two enormous boxes built of reinforced concrete sit one atop the other, connected to the mountainside of one of the 365 small islands that dot the regions of Paraty and Angra dos Reis in Brazil. These low-lying, horizontal elements cantilever 26 feet (8 meters) across the coast and appear to be in perfect proportional balance.

Visitors must arrive by boat and traverse a metal bridge over a still reflecting pool to reach the house. Inside, the living areas and the bedrooms open out to the ocean through a grand aperture that expands across the width of the facade. The upper level of the house is devoted to terraces, an observatory, and gardens for growing medicinal plants and edible herbs.

FOGO ISLAND STUDIOS
2011 | Fogo Island, Newfoundland and
Labrador, Canada

Fogo, an island off the coast of Newfoundland, is an isolated place with an untamed terrain and few residents. A collection of small studios, spread across the island, form the built aspect of a long-term program to cultivate and preserve arts on the islands, and is designed to dignify the wild natural environment while, at the same time, providing a new inspirational beacon for the community.

The largest of these studios, the Long Studio, is divided into three interior zones that reflect seasonal progression. The entrance, representing spring, is a protected open space. The central unit is also open and, of the three, is the most exposed, intended to be inhabited during the long summer days. The rear portion of the studio is fully enclosed, embodying solitude and shelter in colder months while framing the spectacular panoramic views beyond. At this end, the studio is suspended above the ground on columns—a technique sensitively employed so that, in the future, there is capacity for its relocation. Each studio sits jewel-like in the dramatic landscape which surrounds them.

RAINFOREST RETREAT
2014 | Vancouver Island, British Columbia, Canada

Located on the coast of Vancouver Island in British Columbia, this house is both a residential retreat and a studio. Nestled in a grove carpeted with ferns, the building works to engage its surroundings by way of intimately framed views of both the forest and the ocean beyond. By entwining two formal volumes into one, the architects have created a structure with an expansive, deep living area and yet a small, low-impact footprint.

Built from local fir and cedar specifically milled for their warm, distinct grains, the house makes the most of the natural light that filters through the canopy and reaches the forest floor. Large windows provide unique interior light conditions that embrace the abundant shadow as much as the sunlight, while on dark or overcast days, carefully positioned artificial lighting transforms the house into a beacon in the woods.

Overlooking the Whistler Valley in British Columbia, Had-away House is a ski chalet positioned on a wedge-shaped site at the top of a steep slope. The design of the house is dictated by the need to shed considerable amounts of snow during the better part of the year; therefore, its sharply angled sculptural roof both protects the structure and deflects the elements of the location's prevailing weather conditions.

The main level of the house consists of a large living area leading to an outdoor deck that addresses the valley below. In order to bring daylight into the house, a crevice-like aperture runs beneath the highest roof ridge and permeates the entire building. Constructed of steel and infilled with wood, this high-performing structure stands defiantly in the surrounding landscape.

MIDDEN GARDEN PAVILION
2014 | Cape Town, South Africa

Located in Cape Town, Midden Garden Pavilion is built on a gently sloping, terraced landscape. The house playfully challenges notions of outdoors and indoors; it is defined by a series of planes that fold to form a large sheltered dining room without walls. The space can accommodate a large number of people and different activities, with a hearth occupying one end and the other extending out to an open patio with kitchen.

The pavilion was designed to distill the surrounding landscape into a single, integrated geometric space. Although constructed using rough, textured concrete, reminiscent of space hewn from a natural rocky outcrop, it is simple and still. Whether night or day, this daring structure illuminates its natural landscape.

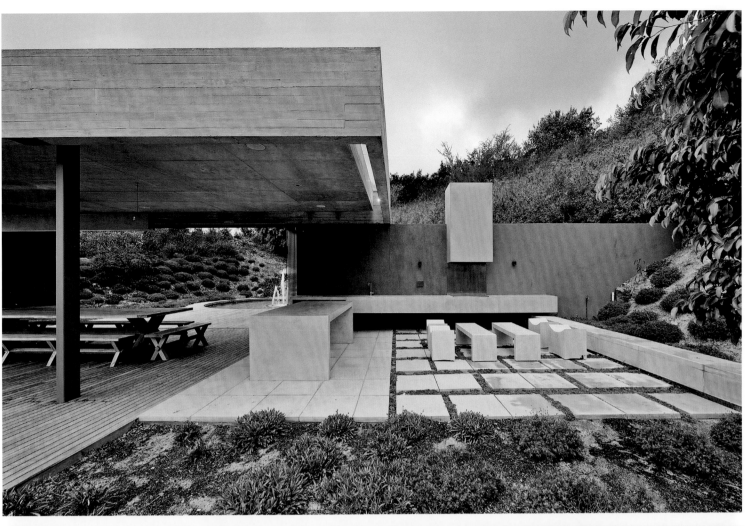

The Water House, located at the foot of Yulong Mountain in Lijiang, China, an ancient trading settlement famed for its network of canals, bridges traditional, symbolic construction techniques and contemporary design. The house is structured around a collection of enclosed courtyards that foster a sense of introspection and draw the eye toward the sky and the peaks of the nearby mountains, just visible above the roofline. At its center is a large, reflective cooling pool bounded by a series of walls and leading pathways. This basin, with water drawn from passing streams, forms the building's reflective heart.

In some respects, this is not a particularly innovative house; its simple timber and glass pavilions, each with a tiled pitched roof, are minimally designed. Instead, the architects have focused on contemplative, atmospheric qualities that serve to emphasize outdoor space and enhance the landscape. Clean and without superfluous ornament, this elegant house defers to its majestic surroundings.

TREEHOUSE SOLLING

2010 | Schönhagen, Uslar, Germany

Rising above a pond near an old forester's abode in a valley clearing in Lower Saxony, Germany, Treehouse Solling gathers together the surrounding woodland, the still water below, and the open skies overhead with an extravagant formal gesture. Initially, a majestic hemlock spruce was chosen as the site, but it was decided that the two-story house should be elevated directly over the pool instead. The structure nevertheless maintains the treehouse idea in its form and with two external staircases, one connecting the two levels of the house and the other descending steeply from a long larchwood deck to the bank below.

The skylight set into the domed roof serves two purposes: to bring in light from above during the day and to observe the starry skies at night. The surrounding landscape teems with life, a natural haven for fish and frogs, as well as deer in the meadows beyond. The building responds to this setting by interacting as quietly with the land as possible. It touches the earth minimally—in the form of slender, reed-like stilts that rise from the water to support the structure above—while reflecting, both literally and otherwise, a heartfelt commitment to enriching the environment for its inhabitants, human and otherwise.

Located on rocky island terrain in Naantali, Finland, the Villa Mecklin is a simple wedge-shaped house created to maximize views across the sea. The residence was built by friends in collaboration with the architects, with design details evolving over the course of a leisurely construction process.

Encompassed by large rocks and low-lying flora and vegetation, the site is a narrow clearing surrounded by tall trees. Clad in untreated wood, the exterior will weather to a gray color over time, reflecting the desire that the house be first and foremost a passive addition to the land. Inside, the house is modest and comfortable. Large doors open onto a deep terrace that stretches to the shore. Wood paneling and white walls ensure the interiors are warm and bright—even on overcast days and dark Finnish nights.

The Alpine Shelter, first conceived in an academic environment at Harvard University, represents the pinnacle of material innovation. Located at an altitude of over 6,562 feet (2,000 meters) in the Slovenian Alps, the bivouac is clad in öko skin fiberglass–reinforced concrete, an extremely light yet strong and durable material that can withstand enormous climactic forces, from wind to snow and landslides. Designed to blend into the surroundings of a rocky environment, the material represents a uniquely conscious approach to concrete construction.

The shelter, which can house eight intrepid mountaineers, is located in an area of unspoiled wilderness, affording rare and spectacular views over the surrounding natural landscape. The dwelling was prefabricated and helicoptered to the site to eliminate the need for its construction to take place on the mountainside, thereby preventing any damage to the ecosystem.

Located on Nova Scotia's Atlantic coast, Cliff House is a simple cubic home perched high on the bedrock overlooking the sea. Four of the building's five elevations face the surrounding landscape; the "fifth," which sits below, presents a unique view from the house to the shoreline. The exterior is clad in cedar shiplap wood, supported by a light steel endoskeleton.

Inside the retreat is a vast living space, akin to a Great Hall, and an open loft above a large cabinet wall. The primary space is paneled in wood, with windows on three sides providing panoramic views across the ocean. The simplicity of the house's design and construction represents a repeatable prototype; several more houses of similar design are planned for the surrounding area.

The Stamp House, located in Queensland, Australia, is a highly technical residence in an otherwise isolated natural setting. Designed to harness nearby resources—water, primarily—in the most efficient and sustainable way, it is set astride an artificial wetland that serves as an engineered water-based ecosystem to support the building. The house itself, a structure of large cantilevers organized around a central core, is composed primarily of concrete, precast and cast in situ.

The cantilevering enables the house to withstand the intense cyclones that strike the region and also protects it from unpredictable and damaging flooding. The roof, completely paneled with solar cells, keeps the house at a constant ambient temperature—a remarkable but necessary achievement for a building of such complexity situated within a climate so extreme.

FARNSWORTH HOUSE
1951 | Plano, IL, USA

Mies van der Rohe's Farnsworth House, located in Plano, Illinois, in a ten-acre secluded woodland close to the meandering Fox River, was completed in 1951 for Dr. Edith Farnsworth as a weekend retreat. It represents one of Modern architecture's earliest attempts to integrate interior space with the landscape.

The entrance to the home is via wide, shallow white stone steps bisected by a platform patio, in keeping with the purity of the building's color scheme and geometry. The slight elevation is functional: as the structure is positioned close to the river, the architect anticipated the periodic flooding that has indeed occurred several times.

The house employs typical Miesian techniques. Eight I beams support the floor slab and the roof at once, providing both the structural engineering and the aesthetic expression. This is a house in which everything is exposed and laid bare: the walls on all four sides are composed almost entirely of glass. While this might ordinarily challenge the need for cooling, shading, and privacy, the architect looked to the surrounding trees for additional protection. This is dwelling in its simplest, and most unifying, sense.

Located in Cachagua, Chile, Casa Ghat is positioned on a steep bank along the coast of the Pacific Ocean. The design of the structure and its spatial arrangement is heavily influenced by this unique topographical condition. The large, concrete roof canopy, angled parallel to the slope of the site, functions as an enormous staircase descending to a viewing platform above the main living area. The irregularly shaped concrete columns that support the structure help delineate the internal spaces of the house and at the same time the spectacular views of the water.

Inside, the organization of the house is less a series of rooms than a topography of varying levels and heights. Two private zones on the upper level, their exteriors clad in wood, emerge from the roof plane like dormers, providing additional means of access to the terrace below.

[2] BUILT WITHIN NATURE

People looking to build once-in-a-lifetime homes often spend years, or even decades, searching for the right site. For houses set in natural landscapes, location is particularly important: it informs and shapes how the building might look, operate, and change over time. These settings are often remote and dramatically beautiful, and they can be very difficult places in which to build. Steep topographies, densely wooded areas, or locales adjacent to large bodies of water present challenges for everything from engineering to weatherproofing to the logistics of transporting construction materials. The designs are often unconventional—either by necessity or as a result of a particular approach by client or architect—and exist in a strong, intimate dialogue with their surroundings. The best, however, challenge their natural environments, either in form or material choice, as the projects assembled in this chapter intelligently demonstrate.

In some instances, the landscape hugs or even envelops the house. In others, abstract interpretations of the formal landscape—such as forests of support columns, reflective exterior paneling, or buildings that undulate in response to their topographical conditions—present beguiling spaces that, while undoubtedly unique, are familiar. Some architects make use of secluded spots to develop quite audacious designs, while others, with an awareness of the structure's visibility in the landscape, begin to quietly yield to the power of what surrounds them.

When faced with a difficult, if not beautiful, landscape, the greatest test is in the process assimilation; it is no simple task to blend a project into its natural environments. Without considerable dedication to the natural processes of the particular site, and a substantial reverence—without too much deference—to the spatial possibilities imbued therein, a building cannot be successfully built *within* nature. In this sense, those collected here are remarkable in their ability to become at one with some of the most demanding landscapes around the world.

Built on a peninsula that stretches south from British Columbia across the border with Canada to Point Roberts, Washington, the Lightbox sits in a dense green woodland beside a park that overlooks creeks, shores, and a large body of water. Designed for a photographer and his family, the home was conceived with an unusually sensitive consideration of light, atmosphere, and detail. Shadows from the surrounding trees dance across its interior walls and floors, while streaks of sunlight patinate the dark, wooden facades. The purity of the light conditions provides all ornament.

Modest in size and simple in form, the building sits in an open dialogue with the surrounding open forest. The architects did not attempt to have the house converge with its surroundings, nor did they seek to have it become "one" with the woodland. Rather, by using affordable and locally crafted materials, they designed it to be both unobtrusive and unassuming; the building meets the ground as lightly as possible, minimizing its footprint. Emphasis, instead, was placed on pulling the landscape into the interior and, in this way, providing a lens through which to appreciate the light, the trees, and the evolving nature of the surrounding clearing.

Karuizawa, a small town near Tokyo, is a popular rural retreat. This villa, perched high on a steep slope in the depths of a forest, embodies the very notion of a hideaway. Built for two musicians who required adaptable interior spaces that could accommodate their domestic needs as well as their collection of contemporary art, the home was designed around the concept of tabula rasa.

Like a primed canvas, its interior is clean and empty. The walls and ceiling are charged white, while the floors are of polished concrete. Warmer materials, such as wood, have been specifically hidden in order to foster the quality of expansiveness and to give the illusion of even larger rooms. The polygonal shape of the building itself, including the roofline, draws the eye in unexpected directions, augmenting the view through large apertures of the green hills beyond.

Rising geometrically from a low-lying field in a hundred-year-old floodplain next to the Methow River, in rural Washington State, the Delta Shelter is a small weekend cabin. The patinated steel of the exterior has a weathered, warm, earth-like coloring. In the words of its architect, it is "a little house in a very large landscape."

As the house is occupied for only part of the year, it was designed to be entirely sealed with enormous sliding steel shutters when not inhabited, creating the impression of a fortress-like observation post for guarding the open meadows. When the house is in use, the shutters can be opened using a manual hand wheel connected to a series of gears and cables to control degrees of light and shade. In this sense, it is a house with a dual personality—generously open in warmer months and protectively closed against less welcome weather conditions when the temperature cools.

Much like an observatory, the Ring House, a dwelling in a forest outside Karuizawa, Japan, near Tokyo, takes command of the landscape. Not constrained by height restrictions, the architects were free to design a building that, like the surrounding trees, reaches to the sky. Although built using traditional techniques, the house plays with conventions in construction; there was no attempt to conflate its striking ringed edifice with its environment.

The interior of the house is deceptively simple: tall, clean, open spaces devoid of all but a few, essential elements and furnishings. The living space is merely suggested by two chairs and a small table; the kitchen is serviced by a simple counter with hooded range. The open, sculptural staircase echoes the rings—dark on the outside, white on the inside—that stripe the glass casing. By minimizing the internal contents, the designers have created a space in which the eye can take in the surrounding woodland at any given moment.

Located in the foothills of the Yarra Valley, northeast of Melbourne, Glenburn House is sited within agricultural land close to a national forest. Positioned at the top of a hill that offers panoramic views, the building is designed to protect its occupants from the often dramatic climatic conditions of the region, including extreme summer heat. The oxidized steel used to clad the exterior reflects the sun and gives the house an earth-colored intensity. The palette carries through to the interior spaces with the use of tallow-wood sealed with orange tung oil on the floors and ceilings, making for a warm and comfortable domestic setting.

Built as an abstracted veranda, the house was specifically designed to leave as small an environmental trace as possible. The building's skin, a grid of very narrow steel slats—like a scrim, or an exoskeleton—not only shades the internal rooms but is equipped to collect solar energy and facilitate the production of hot water. Double-glazed windows allow the house to be passively managed. As water is not easily stored in this region, rainwater is captured and pooled in a tank below ground, the house's only source of water. And the garden has been specifically landscaped using drought-tolerant indigenous vegetation that, much like the house itself, elegantly manages its environment.

Designed to be a sculptural element in the landscape as well as a shelter *from* the landscape, the MIMA Light house defies prototypical conventions in home building. Inspired by the work of Minimalist artists Donald Judd and Robert Morris, the building features a combination of highly polished mirrored planes and large windows, blurring its boundaries. This aesthetic move suggests its suspension both above the fields and between the trees.

The interior spaces, in contrast to the exterior faces, are paneled with richly grained, lacquered pinewood that emanates warmth. The homogenous treatment serves to accentuate the views of the surrounding landscape, framed by floor-to-ceiling apertures at either end and at the middle. The house is designed as a repeatable unit: a dwelling that is self-contained, sustainably operated, and able to be manufactured off-site before being moved to its final location, in whatever landscape that might be. Above all, this home embodies efficient, compact living—in functional, minimalist style.

By studying how the geology of a site might determine its shape over time, the architects of Croft House designed the home to be *from* the surrounding landscape rather than an element on it. Because of their belief that there is an instinctive bond between people and other natural systems, they sought to create a building that, in addition to providing shelter, engages the natural elements. It is a home that embraces its landscape.

Located on the Victorian coast of Australia, the building "turns its collar up" to prevailing easterly winds without completely shielding itself from their effect. Shaped like a sand dune and inspired by the oscillating sine curve, the tapered exterior allows for peripheral views from within, and disguises expansive interior space. Inside, gently curving walls direct the eye outward, creating a lens bisected by the ocean. Much like the water in its midst, this building implies movement.

Located on Long Island, Montauk House is situated in a small valley running adjacent to the Atlantic Ocean. Set within a patch of small trees and bushes next to a sandy beach, the house lies low and monolithic. The sand-colored finish of the exterior makes it feel like an intimate part of its coastal site. The building "deflects in form," in the words of the architect, to engage naturally with the flow of the dunes.

Decks, built from silvered ipe to resemble the dry texture of driftwood, extend out toward the ocean. A collection of vertical planes rise from the roof, designed to frame views and create a balanced counterpoint to the structure's long, horizontal mass. The close relationship between the house and the undulating landscape is underlined by clean, shaded interior spaces and large windows, drawing the focus toward the infinite horizon beyond.

HAYES RESIDENCE

2014 | Berkeley Springs, West Virginia, USA

A building created with simplicity and sensitivity can, in the right conditions, result in a powerful space. The Hayes Residence, sited above the bed of a stream in a forested park near Berkeley Springs, is surrounded by oak and birch trees. The architects have fully embraced this arboreal environment by leaving some of the growth undisturbed: the house actually wraps around a few trunks, which, left exposed behind glass, create the impression of posts supporting the large beams of the vaulted ceilings.

The main house is narrow and unobtrusive, lying low in the woodland. The foundation meets the ground in only two places; the structure of the building hinges from two large trunk-like columns. Patinated copper, slate tiles, and almost continuous walls of glass compose the building's exterior. The rooms within graciously welcome the surrounding forest, showcasing the green of the leaves and the warm brown of the timbers. The house is in quiet dialogue with the landscape it is a part of.

CASA CANDELARIA
2016 | San Miguel de Allende, Mexico

Designed as a succession of well-proportioned volumes, Casa Candelaria—located on the outskirts of San Miguel de Allende, in Mexico—was conceived from the outset to be an integral part of the arid landscape in which it is set. Cactus, mezquite, and huizache blend into terraces, patios, and internal rooms to evoke a feeling of timelessness or, at the very least, the sense that the house has existed for longer than it actually has. Even the very fabric of the building has been constructed from compacted soil from the site itself to emulate the geological layers of the earth.

The living spaces are defined by open circulation; hallways not only connect the rooms of the house but also the outdoor space, comprising an orchard, a greenhouse, and a guest house. This internal arrangement allows for the surrounding valley to be pulled into focus from any room.

The Villa Vals, located on an Alpine slope in Graubünden, Switzerland, is mostly concealed within the earth, hardly visible to passersby. The house is defined by its submersion, yet it has been cleverly designed to leverage spectacular views across the valley. The exposed facade fronts an oval opening excavated from the hill that serves as both an entrance to the home and an outdoor patio. Here, firewood is stored beneath an overhanging lip, and shelter can be taken from the winds that cross the wide open landscape beyond.

The primary entrance to the house is via a warren-like underground tunnel accessed from an adjacent old Graubündner barn. Once inside the Villa, a fluid collection of rooms designed by Bjarne Mastenbroek and Christian Müller is revealed, united by a topography of uninterrupted concrete—floors, walls, ceilings, steps—that homogenizes the interior. Bedrooms are compact, contributing to the sense of the home as true shelter.

Brekkuskógur, in Southwest Iceland, is a landscape of open vistas and broad horizons. Here, near Lake Laugarvatn, a collection of wooden cottages has been nested in the fields to create a semirural residential enclave. Peeking just above the grassline, the buildings are clad in burnt hardwood paneling—using a popular Japanese construction method—creating dark silhouettes in the landscape.

Leftover earth from the site excavation was used to build protective bunkers that shelter the outdoor terraces, while flora and vegetation from the footprint of each building was preserved and replanted on the roofs, referencing vernacular Icelandic turf houses. Inside the cottages, corridors and hallways were kept to a minimum, thereby creating large, open rooms that seem to expand into the surrounding fields. The floors are finished with smooth, highly polished, reflective concrete, while the ceiling panels mimic the external cladding. These houses, through simple techniques, gently contrast with the vast open landscape.

Square House is a weekend home located on a narrow, sloping site in Karuizawa, near Tokyo. Positioned on a ridge at the edge of a mountain dotted with stands of bamboo and tall trees, the house has been designed to "float" in the woodland. The slender columns that support the building extend through the floor and penetrate the living spaces, where they delineate "rooms" defined by their minimal furnishings: daybed, dining table, kitchen counter, bathtub. Windows encircle the entire structure, and a large overhanging roof creates a canopy.

On the side where the building meets the ground, the view is of tree bases, while the opposite side peers above the treeline. The sloping land, the graduation of the surrounding scenery, and the ambiguity of its edges make this house appear both of and above its landscape.

Located in the Indian city of Alibag, this building is woven into a landscape rich in fruit-bearing trees clustered on the banks of a seasonal stream. Built using board-marked textured concrete, the monolithic building is composed of "branches" that have been deformed, stretched, and pushed to frame views and dramatize a series of spatial moments.

In contrast to the dark, heavy exterior, the interior spaces make use of height, space, and light to engage with the surrounding landscape and the site's unique climatic conditions. The entrance veranda and living spaces, for example, are separated from the bedrooms by an open bridge across the stream. A large kitchen at the center of the home has an aperture in the ceiling, flooding the room with natural light and affording a connection to the sky above. This living area, raised above the ground, offers panoramic views of distant mountains. Just outside the house a swimming pool is aligned to the streambed, a celebration of the presence of water during the monsoons and a reminder of the heavy rains during the dry season. Just as water ebbs and flows, the house's structural elements bear a similar level of fluidity.

This house is a contemporary take on one of the oldest types of North American dwellings: the Native American pit house. These structures, sunk partway into the ground for climatic stability, provided comfortable, adaptable living spaces. Edgeland House, excavated seven feet (two meters) into a hillside, has another meaningful connection to the land: it is sited in a location that has been scarred considerably by industry.

Positioned between an existing industrial zone and a river, the house seeks to balance the landscape by, quite simply, extending it. The living spaces are physically divided from the sleeping rooms, requiring inhabitants to pass from one to the other in the open air. This aspect, combined with intelligent mechanical features to ensure sustainable design, lend an impression that the house is deeply integrated within its landscape. Following its completion, more than forty species of native flora were reintroduced to its roof and gardens.

Located in Nasu, Japan, in Tochigi Prefecture, this house—a cluster of tepees, of sorts—lies on a wooded path in a forest grove. The unique tapered outlines of the building respond directly to the tall trees that surround it, while the angled walls represent a careful elimination of unnecessary space.

The building's exterior, which is dark and unobtrusive in nature, belies a bright, white collection of rooms. The interior was crafted to the habits of the occupants, who spend less time at the edges of a room and more in the center. The repeating triangular shapes—doorways, apertures directed toward the forest—create complex, nuanced interiors. At the same time, however, the house was designed with recognition of the limitations of its site; as it is raised slightly above the ground, animals and moisture are prevented from entering. This is a house which provides, above all, shelter from the surrounding landscape.

Sinking homes into the landscape is not an uncommon technique employed by architects. It offers a way to minimize a building's visual impact, especially in sensitive landscapes, and thereby makes it feel a more integrated part of its surroundings. This home, located in Pembrokeshire, Wales, uses this approach—but in a more radical way, as befits a fin de siècle home.

The house itself appears like an eye overlooking the ocean. The only faces visible are two apertures, one the ovoid eye-shape wall of glass panels framed in a stainless steel frame, the other a triangular wedge with a door, opposite. Everything else is concealed beneath the earth, the roof and walls turfed with local vegetation. The roof itself is supported by a steel ring beam that rests on a continuous block wall, enabling a column-free interior living space, which is simply arranged. An open hearth serves as the focus of the house, and the service spaces—the kitchen and the bathroom—are contained in a prefabricated pod. The curved plywood "underbelly" of the roof reflects the soft, undulating shape of both the home and its landscape.

MIMETIC HOUSE

2007 | Dromahair, County Leitrim, Ireland

Mimetic House, positioned in the center of a green, hilly landscape in County Leitrim, Ireland, is prismatic in form, with angled mirrored facades. The building is at once an element in contrast with its surroundings and—due to its reflective characteristics—able, in certain light, to almost become camouflaged against it: a true act of mimesis.

The lower level of the dwelling, where the entrance and the sleeping and study quarters are located, is semi-concealed below ground, accessible by a dip in the landscape. The main living space above is connected by an interior spiral staircase. It is bright and light, with a rhythm of uniformly positioned windows facing the surrounding fields in all directions. The dramatic angular shape of the exterior is felt on the inside, where the eye is drawn up and outward. At the center of the room lie the simple components required for comfortable contemplation of the landscape: a wood-burning stove, a small space for food preparation, and a convivial seating arrangement.

Seen from a distance, this coastal Peruvian house, located a short distance south of Lima, appears like a jagged inscription in the middle of a vast, arid landscape. The site, once Inca territory, is steeply sloped, with mountains on one side and a green valley on the other. The owners fell in love with the location years before commissioning the house, and therefore it represents a profoundly sensitive commitment to the landscape.

The design of the house follows the Peruvian tradition of searching for the *apu*, or "protector," in the surroundings. In so doing, the architects sought to create a balanced dialogue between the architecture and the landscape, blurring the boundaries of what might be defined as interior and exterior space. Stone and concrete cast in situ combine to provide a warm, atmospheric quality throughout, which rests both semidisguised and comfortably settled in its powerful and majestic natural setting.

Passage House, situated in Karuizawa, Japan, in Nagano Prefecture, possesses a powerful yet deferential diagram. The architects, wanting to achieve as much visibility of the landscape as possible, designed a sweeping corridor of a building that juts out from the side of a hill face before looping back to meet it once again, like a horseshoe. The places where the building meets the ground have been minimized, resulting in the impression that the house sticks to the side of the slope.

The interior, determined by its passage-like form and lined end to end with windows on all sides, commands impressive views through the canopy of the trees. It is also instilled with a strong sense of movement, almost cyclical in nature, and reflects the surrounding scenery: mountains and trees within an undulating, verdant terrain. Some of the trees, growing in the gap between the two ends of the structure, appear to extend through the house itself.

[3] BUILT WITH NATURE

Architecture, at its core, is a localized practice: the very first dwellings mankind built were directly born from the earth. Although it's still possible to identify practices that employ ancient modes of building, a more globalized approach has taken hold. Whereas glistening white marble from Carrara can now be found in bathrooms from Hong Kong to California, the projects assembled in this chapter tend to employ materials that bear an explicit relationship to their landscapes—an ambition that often demands both perseverance and expertise.

Designing with nature is no mean feat. It requires, above all, patience and an intimate knowledge of the materials being tamed. Perhaps less obviously, it also requires an element of courage. By subtracting from a landscape in order to create new space, architecture leaves an indelible mark—and one that cannot be easily repaired if a house ultimately sits uncomfortably. In this sense, these projects require a sensitive eye and a measured approach if they are to succeed as new elements in existing environments. Yet with these considerations there remains plenty of room for daring architectural statements, as demonstrated here.

Approaches differ from site to site, client to client. Some projects are consciously assimilated into their landscape, while others actively reinterpret their surroundings. Either way, material choices and the ways in which they are employed sit at the heart of this approach to architecture and, by extension, inform the design considerably. For example, the elemental, inherent properties of stone and wood define the atmospheric and structural qualities of rooms, apertures, and thresholds. In the same way, choosing to build over a stream, falling water, or rocky outcrops bridges a gulf between the landscape and the structure, fusing the two into an architectural statement. In short, these are homes that offer a profound and meaningful engagement with their natural environments.

Located in Utsunomiya, Japan, the House Before House is a dwelling that conflates interior with exterior space. Designed with the premise that people naturally live interstitially, as opposed to only indoors, the house—rather experimental in its conception—operates as a village of sorts. Individual rooms, separate from one another, are nevertheless united by staircases and courtyards to form a spatial continuum.

This labyrinthine series of structures represents a search for harmony between the natural and the man-made. This traditionally Japanese concept of living allows for the house to boldly stand out against its surroundings while incorporating, at various scales, elements of the natural environment. Designed to be timeless, the house intelligently plays with habitual preconceptions of what defines a dwelling, to become far more than a series of interconnected rooms.

The striking red Casa Malaparte stands in splendid isolation atop a cliff facing the Gulf of Salerno on the Italian isle of Capri: it is only reachable by foot or by water. Commissioned by the Italian writer Curzio Malaparte, who collaborated with the architect, the building represents a hybrid of Modern architecture and classical elements—a postmodern building realized far before its time. Using a particular approach to geometry and aesthetics, the house appears resilient against the natural landscape while maintaining sensitivity toward it.

Built with stone extracted from the site, the house appears to have grown from the landscape. On one side, the roof of the long, narrow structure takes the form of a wedge-shaped brick staircase ascending to a solarium, contributing to the impression that the house is an extension of, rather than an addition to, the cliff. Here one encounters the full drama of the infinite ocean horizon. Within the interior, a more conventional spatial arrangement accommodates fluid circulation from one room to another, creating a sense of freedom. A private apartment, designed for Malaparte's private use, projects proudly out toward the seascape—like a beacon, anchored firmly in the rock.

Located in the Australian territory of Victoria, Earth House sits amid an extensive coastal property. Designed to align with the rural characteristics of the surrounding environment, the house makes use of expansive sightlines across a gently undulating landscape. The building appears to rise from the earth as if of the earth; one side, the western elevation, is without any doors or windows at all. Constructed using rammed earth and local Dromana crushed rock, this monolithic structure stakes a decisive claim on the landscape.

Inside, a series of individual modules contain the living spaces and sleeping areas, all connected by one long corridor described by the architects as a "disappearing street." This elongated service space plays with light, shade, and the external views. At the center of the compound is a large open courtyard, protected from the prevailing winds and drawing sunlight into the core of the home. Here, visually separated from the main house, is a self-contained living space which is in fact connected by a windowed walkway that also serves a panoramic viewing deck, which stands above a botanical labyrinth at the heart of the property.

Located at the foot of the Qinling Mountains in China, this house very clearly derives from the surrounding landscape. Thousands of small rocks from the nearby river, carefully arranged by size, shape, and color, are set within a minimal concrete framework forming the house's primary structure. A small doorway in the perimeter leads to a courtyard with a reflective pool.

The interior, a collection of sparse, open spaces that provide simple circulation, is lined in plywood with an intricately patterned bamboo veneer, evoking a traditional Chinese domestic atmosphere. Both the ground-floor living area and the second level are faced on one side with floor-to-ceiling glass panels that open out to the courtyard; louvered shutters, faced with the same patterned veneer seen throughout the dwelling, can be shut to provide privacy.

DRAGSPEL HOUSE

2004 | Smolmark, Årjäng, Sweden

Dragspel House, a contemporary extension to a cabin dating back to the nineteenth century, is located on the shore of Lake Övre Gla in the Glaskogen Nature Reserve in Sweden. The building is an intelligent response to a series of complex and strict building regulations. Used for only two months of the year, the house remains closed, as if in deep hibernation, during cold months. When summer comes, the house opens out onto the shore of the lake, breathing once again, like a bear emerging from its den.

The extension, clad in an undulating pattern of red cedar shingles that will fade, over time, to the monochromatic gray tones of the surrounding rocks, is at once bold and passively integrated with its dense woodland landscape. The structure employs a rib-cage design, and the interior walls and ceiling of the remarkably organic, warren-like den are lined with pine lattice and reindeer hides to create a cozy, typically Nordic atmosphere.

Frank Lloyd Wright's Fallingwater, in the Bear Run Nature Reserve, outside Mill Run, Pennsylvania, sits at a point where a mountain stream flowing almost 1,300 feet (396 meters) above sea level breaks to descend 30 feet (9 meters) over cascading rock. Commissioned by the Kaufmann family to construct a spacious country retreat, the architect was at total odds with their concept of a house facing the waterfall; he envisioned—and subsequently realized—a "floating" building that is both embedded into and suspended above the falling water below.

The house, completed in 1939, is composed of two buildings: the house over the water and a smaller guest house farther up the bank, connected by a winding pathway. The stacked, interlocking volumes of the main house—each designed to have a specific relationships to the surrounding natural elements—belie the simplicity of its interior.

The very presence of the falls permeates every aspect of the home. Even when the water is not visible, its constant, tumbling rhythm resonates acoustically, while boulders embedded in the waxed stone floors suggest a shallow stream meandering gently through its rooms. More conspicuously, a staircase behind a glass opening, descending from the main living space, allows access to a secluded bathing spot below the cantilevered terraces.

HOUSE IN THE OUTSKIRTS OF BRUSSELS
2007 | Brussels, Belgium

This two-story suburban dwelling, three sides of which are fully covered in rich flora and vegetation, is an extension to the existing home of an artist. The fourth side of the building is a wall of windows shielded by enormous translucent white polyester curtains that provide both shade and privacy. The structure's flamboyant exterior belies a more traditional internal arrangement.

The composition of exotic greenery, selected by botanical artist Patrick Blanc, is rooted directly into a felt surface that extends to and expands across the roof. Intelligent engineering was required to ensure the house could support the weight of the installation and remain watertight. Built-in irrigation and fertilization systems provide for constant care of the plants.

Aloni, located on the Greek island of Antiparos, in the Cyclades, is a house firmly of its site. Set into the incline of a coastal hill, the dwelling also pays homage to the domestic traditions and techniques that prevail on the rural island. In a part of the world being shaped in ever increasing ways by holiday homes, this building is in some ways reactionary. Dry rubble stone walls, commonly used in agriculture to create arable plateaus, enclose the house on two sides and bridge two hills. In the resulting small valley is the living area.

With its mass disguised by the land, the actual size of the house cannot be discerned by passersby. Four small courtyards divide the internal spaces into five zones. This arrangement allows for multiple vistas of the ocean and for natural daylight to flood the space without sacrificing protection from the elements.

Oscar Neimeyer's Casa Canoas, located in Rio de Janeiro, is an exemplar of innovative open-plan living. The single-story house, topped by an organic, sinuous flat roof, is composed almost entirely of windows. Enclosed by a forest, and with occasional views out to the ocean beyond, the house builds upon the architectural ideas of Modernists like Le Corbusier, but with a prototypical Latin American sensibility.

A granite boulder embedded in the ground stands in contrast to the orthogonal lines and flat planes of the house and gardens. Inside becomes outside, and visa versa, creating the sensation that the rooms extend outward into the surrounding jungle. Less of a house and more of a pavilion, the Casa Canoas seeks to reorder its natural context by refocusing the landscape and drawing it into a protected, sheltered environment. The white plane of the slender roof appears to slice through the canopy of the trees to address the clearing and, in one gesture, presents a system for elegant living.

M2 Hill House is a prototype designed to engage with a particular landscape wherever it might be located: it is nomadic by nature. From a distance, the house appears to be no more than a hilly mound in the earth—its turf-covered roof, which slopes to the ground on two sides, blends naturally with the green of its agricultural surroundings. Designed, in the words of its architects, to appear to have "grown from its context," the building playfully oscillates between man-made structure and perceived natural environment. Coupled with a simple structural system, the materials deployed are purposely common and abundant so that the house can be constructed all over the world.

The roof of M2 Hill House is layered with sedum, a robust genus of leaf succulent. Beneath this canopy, the internal spaces are ordered by two walls: one of glass, affording views of rolling hills, and the other of wood, defining the house's sleeping and service spaces. Its inherent simplicity is intended to satisfy a demand for flexibility while enriching its green, open surroundings.

Swiss artist Not Vital has erected a daring and defiant house at the edge of an island in General Carrera Lake in Chilean Patagonia. Carved directly from an enormous white marble outcrop, it is one continuous material element. Partially obscured, it has the appearance, in the words of the artist, of a "hidden monolithic sculpture." When illuminated at night, it looks like a lighthouse from across the water.

A large domed ceiling dominates the interior spaces. Ornamentation is delivered solely through different treatments of the marble: polished smooth, revealing the vein, or left in its roughly hewn state. From the central area it is possible to see both ends of the structure, with apertures positioned to capture views of both the sunset and the moonrise.

A long, snaking tunnel leads from the main building at the edge of the shore up through the rock itself toward a rectangular aperture on the opposite side of the island. This space is dark and roughly carved to evoke a sense of disorientation; employing a spatial trick known as "reward and denial," the view at the climax of the procession is thereby made particularly magnificent. Perhaps more sculptural than functional, the house can be considered an inhabitable piece of art; it's designer qualifies any sculpture in which one can stand, sit, or sleep as a dwelling.

This is a house built with, from, and into rock. Located in the San Juan Islands in Washington State and overlooking a bay of the Salish Sea, the Pierre is nestled within a large stone outcrop, rather than beside or astride it, accentuating its orthogonality in an otherwise organic setting. From certain angles, the house almost appears to disappear into the surrounding landscape.

The building's construction was necessarily complex. The rock, integral to the material language of the house, required special care to ensure no unwanted fractures.

Because of this, the design of the home required a degree of flexibility. The main spaces are defined by concrete walls and large thresholds, together forming a series of interlocking volumes that—while undoubtedly distinct—sit comfortably next to the still, reflective plane of the water.

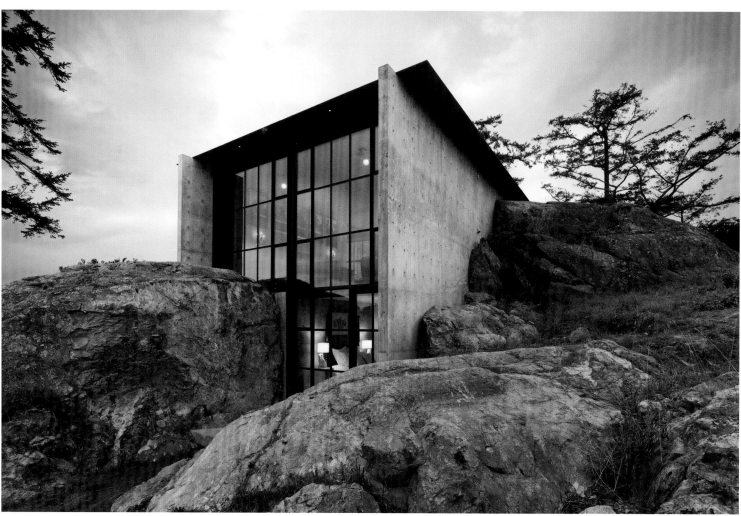

BJELLANDSBU HUNTING LODGE
2013 | Etne, Hordaland, Norway

The Bjellandsbu Hunting Lodge, located beside a lake in the untouched mountains close to Åkrafjorden, in the western part of Norway, appears to emerge from its setting, a majestic rocky landscape layered with green grasses and heathers. Although modest in size, it can comfortably accommodate twenty-one people—as long as they have arrived by foot or on horseback.

The roof, covered in grass, rises elegantly from one side of the house and swoops down the other to reach the ground, contributing to its appearance of just another natural element of the landscape. It is supported by two curved steel beams that define the hut's interior, a single open space organized around a central hearth. A glass wall and windows frame the landscape on two sides. The construction materials, local stone and wood treated with tar, create a dialogue between contemporary expression and more vernacular building techniques. Viewed from afar, the cabin is almost entirely disguised amid the pools, crevices, and canyons of the surrounding landscape: only the stark concrete chimney indicates an island of human habitation.

Moledo House, located outside Porto, responds boldly to its complex and strict natural stone environment with the architect's characteristic sensitivity. The concrete slab roof, the most visible plane of the building, has been designed to appear like a totally new element in the landscape—as if it had fallen from the sky.

The design of the house was gradually refined over a seven-year building process. In order to support the building, the existing hillside was reshaped to create a series of terraced stone retaining walls and platforms. The unassuming exterior, masked on one side by the walls and open to a valley on the other, contains a modest, elegant set of interior spaces rhythmically arranged and paneled in wood.

Located in suburban Westchester County, north of New York City, Pound Ridge House sits amid 33 acres (13 hectares) of rocky terrain and woodland. The clients, who sought to bring the feeling of the forest inside the house, requested a "house in the woods, of the woods." The reflective volumes that compose the house are set onto a plateau of clearings that, according to the architects, had the rooms almost naturally inscribed into its surface.

The house is set at the end of a long driveway that snakes along the contours of the land. The meandering journey continues inside the structure itself, which folds to accommodate a cluster of large boulders. Rooms take the form of large, open, and fluid spaces. The exterior is clad in various materials that reflect seasonal shifts and the ever changing nature of the site: stainless steel (both brushed and polished), tin–zinc–coated copper, and glass, mirroring the surrounding landscape in a singularly contemporary gesture.

The Tolo House, located in Lugar das Carvalhinhas, in Alvite, Portugal, is a holiday home. Built on a narrow, sharply sloping site, the house is arranged as a cascade of stepped terraces to best capture sunlight and the view, bringing a highly unusual geometric element to the landscape. The structure can be accessed by a pathway from the the bottom and a road at the top.

The exposed concrete structure adapts naturally to the topography of the site, evoking enormous stones or, in a sense, a solid monolith. Clean, white living spaces unfold as a series of compartmentalized rooms that align to the structure of the house. A staircase ascends the length of the exterior, providing access to the pebbled terraces on the roof of each unit. Directly beneath it lies another stairway, forming the sole route for navigating the interior and corresponding precisely to the uniquely fragmented, yet holistic, form of the building.

Located in Sandefjord, Norway, Cabin Knapphullet is a small extension to an existing property by the sea. Occupying a small footprint, the structure houses a compact living area, a sleeping loft, and a bathroom. Accessed by a footpath that winds along a woods-edged meadow, the house is defined by its unusual roof, which folds to form a wide staircase of shallow steps connecting its viewing platform to the ground below.

As the house is built against large boulders and dense vegetation, natural light is intentionally drawn into the interior through various apertures, including a slit in the roof. The wood slats that line the ceiling and sawn oak wall panels lend warmth to the environment, offsetting the coolness of the polished concrete floors and the austere rock formations outside, dramatically fronted by walls of glass.

Located in Nagano Prefecture, the Too Tall Teahouse is a tiny dwelling perched precariously on top of two large tree trunks soaring above a ridge in the middle of a woodland. The building has only one room with one purpose: to make and consume tea in a space conducive to viewing, and reflecting upon, the natural surroundings and the urban center beyond.

The compact teahouse, clad with timber and tree bark and punctured with three apertures, is accessible only by ascending wooden ladders and entering through a hatch in the floor. While a number of surrounding trees were tactically removed to open up the landscape and enhance the vistas, the house sits comfortably in its setting. A steeply pitched roof shelters the house from the elements.

Casa Meztitla is embedded in the uniquely impressive natural landscape of Tepoztlán, Mexico, close to El Tepozteco National Park. In order for the house to be easily maintained, its material composition is simple: a concrete structural base and walls made of a compound of volcanic rock, cement blocks, white cement, and lime render.

The house's arrangement provides a continuous engagement between the interior spaces and the landscape. The rooms are connected by a diverse series of outdoor spaces: one cannot go from one area to another without walking through the open air, a feature enabled by the benign subtropical climate. This symbiotic relationship is further expressed with walls of large, pivoting glass doors, giving the option of converting indoor space to outdoor space and emphasizing the sense of being always open to the surroundings.

Located in Karjat, Maharashtra—a short drive from Mumbai—the Riparian House sits at the heart of a mountainous UNESCO World Heritage Site: the Western Ghats. The natural landscape transforms from a pale grassy flatland to a dense, bright green, jungle-like forest during the summer monsoon. The house has been carefully articulated to harness the best views of the landscape in all seasons.

The living spaces are spread across the length of the building, which culminates in a submerged courtyard enclosed by limestone walls. A screen of uniformly spaced bamboo poles along the front of the house provides privacy without disrupting views of the landscape, facilitating a special dialogue between the enclosed spaces of the house and the expansive territory beyond.

———

Page references for illustrations
appear in **boldface**.

Phaidon Press Limited
Regent's Wharf
All Saints Street
London N1 9PA

Phaidon Press Inc.
65 Bleecker Street
New York, NY 10012

phaidon.com

First published 2016
© 2016 Phaidon Press Limited

ISBN 978 0 7148 7317 6

A CIP catalogue record for this book is available from the
British Library and the Library of Congress.

Commissioning Editor: Emilia Terragni
Project Editor: Laura Loesch-Quintin
Production Controller: Mandy Mackie
Design: Studio Joost Grootens/Joost Grootens,
    Dimitri Jeannottat, Julie da Silva
Text: James Taylor-Foster

Printed in China

The publisher would like to thank Tanya Heinrich, Valerie
Saint-Rossy, Susan Clements, and Sarah Smithies for their
contributions to the book.